THE
First Words
Picture Book

Bill Gillham

Photographs by
Sam Grainger

COWARD-McCANN, INC.
NEW YORK

dog

Jenny is giving the dog his dinner.

ball

John and Jenny are throwing the ball.

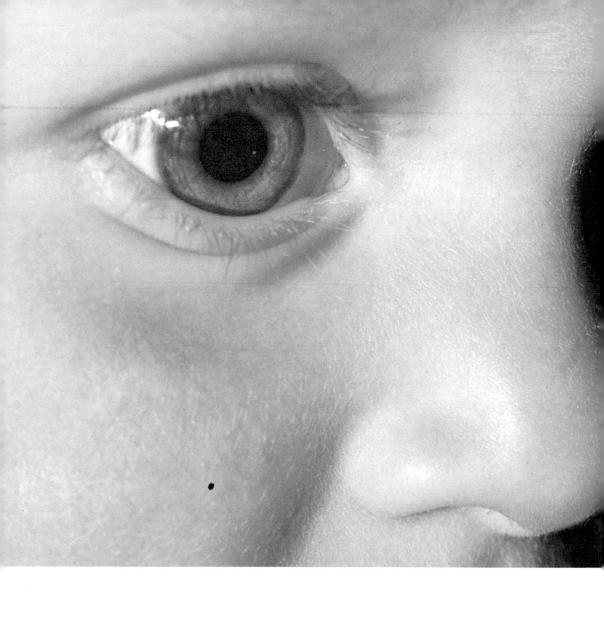

eye

Jenny and her mommy play peekaboo.
Jenny is covering her eyes.

book

Mommy is reading a book to the children.

shoes

John helps Mommy to clean his shoes.

clock

Jenny shows John the numbers on the clock;
they can hear it go tick-tock, tick-tock.

car

Mommy puts gas in the car.

spoon

John and Jenny eat their pudding with a spoon.

horse

Daddy gives the horse an apple.

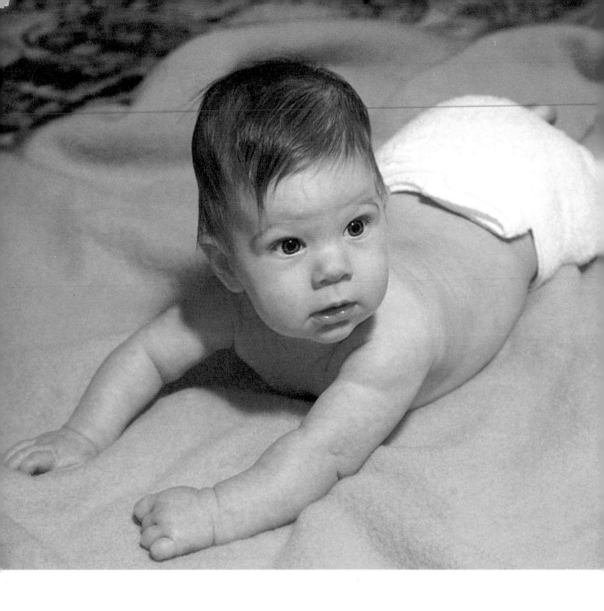

baby

The baby likes her bottle.

bird

John and Jenny keep very still;
they don't want to frighten the bird.

drink

Jenny is thirsty; she's having a drink.

bath

John and Jenny are playing in the bath.

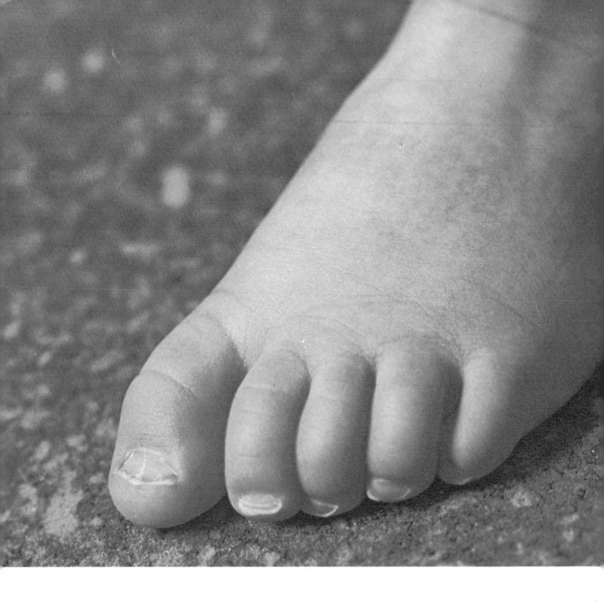

toes

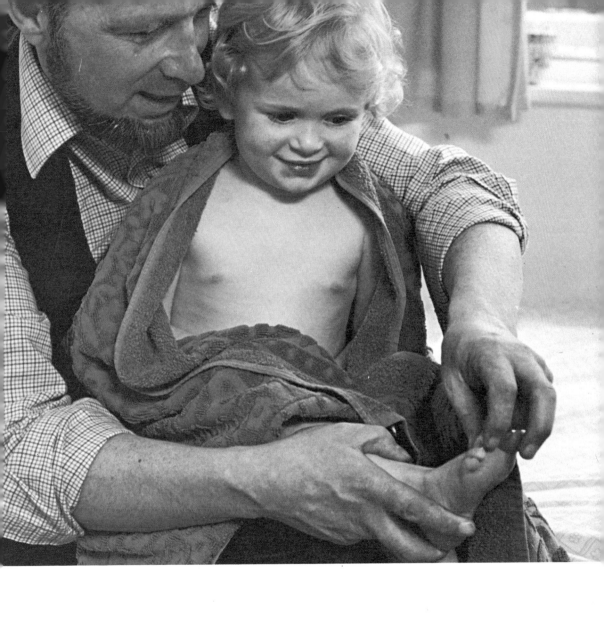

Daddy plays 'This little piggy' with Jenny's toes.

teddy bear

John and Jenny take their teddy bears to bed.

What do children talk about when they start to speak? Research carried out at the University of Nottingham and Harvard University has resulted in *The First Words Picture Book*, presenting the fifteen topics that occur most often in children's first words. Each topic is shown by itself and then "in action," by superb color photographs. All have a special fascination for children and provide a powerful stimulus to developing their language. Talking around the pictures, as well as naming them, and asking questions such as "What are they doing? What's the little girl holding in her hand? What do you think will happen next?" helps to extend children's language, as well as increasing their pleasure in a book that is based on what *children* are interested in.

Text copyright © 1982 Bill Gillham
Photographs copyright © 1982 Sam Grainger
First American Edition 1982
First published by
Methuen Children's Books Ltd., London, England

Library of Congress Cataloging in Publication Data
Gillham, Bill. The first words picture book
Summary: Simple words such as dog, ball, shoes,
and clock are used in sentences and illustrated
with photos.
1. Vocabulary—Juvenile literature, [1. Vocabulary]
I. Grainger, Sam, ill.   II. Title.
PE 1449.G45   1982   428.1   81–12452
ISBN 0-698-20560-X   AACR 2
ISBN 0-698-20605-3 pbk.

Second Impression
Second Impression (pbk.)
First Paperback Edition 1984
Printed in the United States of America